Here in are pictures of fog &
Rain

Mountain & the shore,
even some hiking

Fortunally — even though there is
one of fishing —

Never a one of a fish

Maybe we'll have better luck
Next time

love Roger
Ei — Megan — Chas
& Janie

THE OLYMPIC PENINSULA

Photography by Tom and Pat Leeson
Introduction by Robert Steelquist
Foreword by Senator Daniel J. Evans

SKYLINE
PRESS

Produced by Roger Boulton Publishing Services, Toronto
Designed by Fortunato Aglialoro

© 1984 Oxford University Press (Canadian Branch)
SKYLINE PRESS is a registered imprint of Oxford University Press

ISBN 0-19-540606-0

1 2 3 4 – 7 6 5 4

Printed in Hong Kong by Scanner Art Services, Inc. Toronto

FOREWORD

Two hundred years ago a British fur trader, John Meares, first glimpsed a glistening white peak rising from a jumble of mountains stretching across the horizon. He named it 'Mount Olympus' after the mountain home of the Greek gods, and Captain Vancouver, a few years later, ratified the choice with great enthusiasm.

The mountains slumbered untouched for the next hundred years. Indian legends of great central valleys teeming with game finally awakened the curiosity of early settlers. Less than one hundred years ago, the first serious explorers penetrated the wilderness. They reported no central valley but rank on rank of mountain peaks stretching in all directions, girded by forests as impenetrable as an Amazon jungle.

President Theodore Roosevelt recognized the unique beauty of this peninsula and declared much of it a National Monument. By the time President Franklin Roosevelt signed legislation establishing the Olympic National Park, the first trickle of recreational hikers started their own explorations. Boy Scouts, mountaineers and future Mt Everest climbers were to first experience the joy of wilderness among these peaks.

I have visited scores of the ocean beaches, hiked virtually every river valley, and climbed most of the Olympic Mountains during the past 45 years. Each visit is a return pilgrimage to a mountain paradise only gently touched by human hands. Vivid technicolor memories recall, instantly, the serenity and savagery of wilderness mountains.

—Summer afternoons in emerald meadows afire with a wildflower rainbow.

—Hot, dusty climbs to ridge tops where cool breezes sing and glistening mountain peaks rise from the nest of valley fog.

—Watching, hushed, as huge Roosevelt elk pick their delicate way over steep rocky slopes.

—Numbingly cold dancing water, hurrying to the sea, offering a drink the equal of the ambrosia of Olympian Gods.

—Lying quietly beside a high lake tuning each sense to the exquisite sounds, odors and touch of nature's world.

The National Park which dominates the Olympic Peninsula has preserved a wilderness land virtually untouched by human habitation. In an increasingly technological and crowded world it is essential that we preserve these windows to the past. Our great grandchildren who may explore the stars must know their heritage and what their world was like before humans came.

As you visit the Olympics through the glorious photography of this book, I hope you will be stimulated to visit and personally enjoy this magnificent land.

United States Senate,
Washington, D.C.,
March 1984

DANIEL J. EVANS

INTRODUCTION

'I could not possibly believe that any uncultivated country had ever been discovered exhibiting so rich a picture. . . .' From the broad back of Protection Island, Captain George Vancouver was looking at the Olympic Mountains, snowy and distant, above rolling foothills covered with thick forests. The year was 1792. After a voyage that had brought him eastward across the Pacific to a landfall in Sir Francis Drake's 'New Albion' and a passage into the fabled Strait of Juan de Fuca, Vancouver was feasting his eyes on a new world—one of incomparable beauty.

It is not surprising that he turned to pictorial analogy in describing the new land that rose before him. The subtle hues of the dark forests, the distant crags of the Olympic summits, and the evanescent coastal fogs, must have presented a composition unlike anything he had seen before. After the level horizons of months at sea this new skyline was jumbled and broken, spires upon ridges upon hills. Unlike the polished gems that are the British Isles, this landscape was unruly and uncultivated; unlike the vivid tropics, ablaze with equatorial light, this scene was muted and soft. Laid out before him was a new visual order, the paradox of a Nature that was at once serene and welcoming, yet wild and forbidding.

In the years that I have lived and worked in the Olympics, this juxtaposition of contrasts remains the most vivid of my impressions. A pass, bathed in late September sun, ripe with the sweetest of the low-bush huckleberries, invites me to stay, regardless of the distance to camp. Moments later the same pass is choked with a cold fog. The vivid red foliage of autumn is washed over by a soft white screen of mists. This is no place in which to stay for long; the welcome has worn thin. Startled by the sudden chill, I shoulder my pack and start down the switchback. As I stop shivering, the sweet aftertaste of the berries returns to my lips.

That images of the Olympics contrast so sharply is testimony to the amazing variety the Olympics present—of landforms and lifeforms and, surprisingly for an area so small, of climate itself. Tacked onto the northwest corner of Washington State, and surrounded on three sides by salt water, the Olympic Peninsula is like a continent in miniature, holding within itself several extremes. Moisture-laden winds from the cold North Pacific pour over 160 inches of rain annually on the fog-bound rain forest valleys of the Quinault, the Queets and the Hoh Rivers and then, as these winds rise over the peaks of the mountain range, they leave more of their rain and snow behind to nourish the glaciers and hasten the freshets of every water-course; but blowing on eastward they dry out completely and cast a 'rain shadow' to the northeast of the mountains, where annual precipitation can measure a scant 15 inches—the lowest level on the west coast. Rivers that rise in the blue mouths of glaciers gather strength as they tumble through the upper canyons of great valleys, and then spread out in broad floodplains as they cross the lowlands to the sea; yet often the distance from terminal morraine to brackish estuary will be less than thirty miles. On beaches around the rim of the Peninsula, shorebirds forage among the drifted kelp for sand fleas; yet within a few miles, golden eagles are soaring above alpine meadows, looking for marmot pups. In the lush rain forests of the west side, Sitka spruce tower 225 feet above the dark and moist forest floor; yet on the sparse, tundra-like, subalpine meadows of the high country, dwarf willows attain a height of only two or three inches, their tops not even emerging above the carpet of summer wildflowers. Such are some of the contrasts, some of the extremes, to be found in this comparatively small area.

Although relatively young in the perspective of geological time, the Olympics can claim a dignified 50 million years of age. Sandstones formed by sediments deposited on the bottom of a shallow sea were covered by flowing basalt that extruded out of ocean-floor volcanic fissures to form undersea mountains called sea-mounts. The spreading action of the sea-floor pushed these ancient beds to the east where they collided with the North American continent and some of the rock, distorted into massive folds, was heaped up over the surface. (Some was forced under the edge of the continent in a process called subduction and heat generated by the friction of subducting rock is thought to be the driving force of the Cascade volcanoes including Mount St Helens.) Over millions of years the ancient sea-bed, with its folds and sea-mount chain, was forced up thousands of feet and so the Olympics were created.

Glaciers advancing from Canada and off the Olympic mountain slopes played the next role in shaping the mountains familiar to us today. 3,000-feet-thick ice chiseled through the coastal lowlands, cutting out Hood Canal, Puget Sound and the Strait of Juan de Fuca. Glacial debris, boulders and cobbles, transported from hundreds of miles to the north, was heaped around the flanks of the range. The basins of Lake Ozette and Lake Crescent were hollowed out by the continental glaciers. Ice blocked the outlets of the northern river valleys, forming ice-choked fiords that backed up into the range, sometimes spilling over the passes to the south.

The little glaciers on the Olympic peaks have also seen periods of advance, shaping river valleys into broad 'U's and sharpening the steep horns of mountain peaks as their freezing action broke the bedrock, lifting and carrying it downward. The runoff of glacier-melt streams runs cloudy with nickel-colored rock flour as the worn Olympics return to the sea.

In the 10,000 years since the last continental glaciers retreated, plant and animal life-forms have re-established their niches in a constant flux of environmental change. Some plants managed to survive the Ice Age on outcrops, islands of rock peaks in a sea of glacier ice. Isolated from their relatives, these plants adapted to unique conditions in the Olympics. They include Flett's violet, Piper's bellflower, Webster's senecio and the magenta painted-brush.

Dry periods saw the advance of pines and juniper to areas high in the mountains. Oaks and cactus, madrona and manzanita spread into the lowlands. Prairie and dryland remnants survive now only in small patches—windows to a semi-arid past.

The abundance of moisture along the coast favored the growth of some of the most productive forests of the Northern Hemisphere. Damp rain forests of spruce, hemlock and cedar, as well as bigleaf and vine maple and red alder, choke the western Olympic river valleys. Here club-mosses and ferns glean nutrients from the moist air as they hang in dense garlands from the limbs of ancient maples. The forest, a vast living tissue, absorbs the buffeting raindrops, and holds the moisture captive in its trunks, limbs, leaves and needles, and in its cool shade.

Higher in the mountains, it is dryness that has shaped the mosaic of forest and meadow. Vast natural tracts of even-aged Douglas fir owe their existence to centuries of drought- and fire-cycles. Incapable of thriving in the shade of other trees, Douglas fir quickly thrives in the aftermath of catastrophic blowdowns and burns. The seeds germinate well in disturbed soil and the seedlings quickly dominate any recent clearing.

Subalpine meadows are also products of Olympic wildfire, coupled with the effects of lingering snowpatches. As the spring melt transforms the alpine blanket into islands of snow and eventually into rivulets of cold water, wildflower communities sprout, bloom, seed and wither. Their growing season is short and delicately balanced, beginning when enough light penetrates the snow cover for them to sprout, and ending when the soil moisture evaporates and they wither from drought. A subtly changing tapestry of mountain flowers across the meadows reflects the gradual advance of the seasons with spring, summer and fall sometimes being separated by only a few yards.

Also evolving in the aeons of gradual transformation in the

Olympics were the animal forms—the fishes of the rivers, lakes and bogs, the elk of the forests and mountains, the small mammals and their predators and even the decomposers that recycle everything once living back into the humus of the earth.

The isolating intervention of glacier ice and bodies of lowland water played a key role in determining which animal species would occur in the Olympics. The so-called 'missing eleven' includes grizzly bears, wolverines, mountain sheep, porcupines and pikas, animals that are now or once were common in the Cascades, but that presumably never reached the Olympics. A total of about 60 mammal species did come to the Olympics, including the Roosevelt elk, the cougar, and the wolf, which has been extinct since the 1920's. Black bears are common, their numbers dependent on the supply of spawned-out salmon, which they scavenge. Several indigenous mammals occur in the Olympics, among them the Olympic marmot and the Olympic chipmunk.

About 260 species of birds find their way to the Olympics—either as permanent residents or as migrating visitors. The endangered spotted owl lives in the dark old-growth forests. Bald eagles pick at the carcasses of spent salmon on gravel bars along the rivers. In the forests, winter wrens rear their tiny nestlings secretly under downed logs, and warblers and hordes of pine siskins feed noisily, high in the forest canopy.

Emerging from the spawning gravels of many of the Olympic rivers, salmon and steelhead trout begin journeys that take them halfway around the North Pacific, and then return to the waters of their origins to perpetuate their kind. These sea-running fish form a critical link in terrestrial as well as aquatic food chains.

The great land-locked trout of Lake Crescent, the Beardslee trout and the Crescenti trout, were renowned for their beauty, size, and fighting skill. Early in this century they attracted the attention of the angling world, Lake Crescent becoming as magnetic as a bonanza lode. A few of these elusive giants remain, their blue backs reflecting the startling azure of the deep.

The human record in the Olympics goes back a long way, to the hunters of hairy elephants in the shadows of receding glacier ice, and to the more recent hunters of whale, seal and salmon—the people of the Cedar Culture. In modern times explorers sensed the promise of the region's resources and settlers rapidly peopled the forests, prairies and harbors, eager to earn their place in America's destiny.

In the Olympics that destiny found fulfilment. Settlement of the American continent reached the Pacific limit here and turned back into itself. At this edge, the best remains balanced between a recent memory of boundlessness and a modern acceptance of the finite. The skills appropriate to this place, the use of unique materials and tools, a wisdom learned on the land, these continue to guide us, together with the lessons learned from the loss of treasures elsewhere.

The Olympic Peninsula retains its full measure of contrasts, a full stock of images that answer our need to balance the terrible with the serene, the brief with the enduring, and the infinity of nature with the diminutiveness of ourselves.

The visual order of the Olympics—richer by far than the glimpses that so impressed Captain Vancouver—emerges and takes shape in the pages that follow. It is a harmony of lush greens redolent with the scent of rain; of vivid sunsets mirrored off a close ocean; of stolen glimpses of elk on a frosted river bar; of horses grazing in the shadow of mountains. It is alpenglow warming the glaciers of Mt Olympus or the velvet of a young buck's antlers; dewdrops lining the soft coat of a fawn or magnifying the sporecap of a moss. It is a natural order in which men may acquiesce without surrender, a Nature generous and close, where the familiar is always changing and where unexpected riches will reward the patient explorer.

Olympia, Washington,   ROBERT STEELQUIST
January, 1984

1 Rhododendron-lined pathways brighten
the way and lighten the load for backpackers
hiking in the Olympic National Forest.

2 Found in mountain meadows during June and July, Jeffrey shooting stars (*Dodecatheon jeffreyi*) capture the attention of even the most casual observer. Elk and deer eat the plant in early spring when green foliage is scarce.

3 *(right)* At their fullest blossom in May and June, rhododendrons (*Rhododendron macrophyllum*) line many of the roads and trails on the Peninsula's drier east side. This beautiful wild shrub is Washington's state flower.

4 Many of the numerous waterways of the wet, western side contain small, unnamed cataracts such as this tributary of the Quinault River.

5 *(right)* Month-old black-tail deer fawns (*Odocoileus hemionus*) bound through alpine meadows carpeted with lupine and bistort. Black-tails are the only species of deer found on the Peninsula and are commonly seen in the summer near Hurricane Ridge and Deer Park.

6 As the highest peak on the Peninsula, Mt Olympus received its name in 1788 from the British ship's captain, John Meares, who thought it a worthy home for the gods. Here viewed from the north on the High Divide, its glaciers and snow fields are accented by delicate white avalanche lilies.

7 A view of the northern Cascade mountain range across fog-covered
Puget Sound from the Hurricane Ridge Road.

8 Subalpine firs (*Abies lasiocarpa*) grow in distinctive clusters in the Olympic subalpine zone. The erect conical form sheds the winter snowloads.

9 Mountain goats (*Oreamnos americanus*) were introduced to Olympic National Park in the 1920's. This is now one of the better goat-viewing areas in the world, where hikers have the opportunity to spy a solitary male or a small nanny band atop a rocky cliff.

10 The setting sun slips behind Point of Arches on the northern Washington coast. Wild and rugged, this strip of coastline is one of the most recent additions to Olympic National Park.

11 *(right)* Fog swirling in from the Strait of Juan de Fuca covers the Morse Creek valley. Klahhane Ridge and Mount Angeles are silhouetted against the sky.

12 *(left)* Covered in a dozen feet of snow, Hurricane Ridge is a winter wonderland.

13 Hoh Lake, one of many such gems tucked into the Olympic mountainscape.

14 One of the twenty indigenous wildflowers found in Olympic National Park, the Fletts violet (*Viola flettii*) grows only on rocky, alpine ridges where it may be seen blooming in mid-summer.

15 *(right)* Broadleaf lupine (*Lupinus latifolius* var. *subalpinus*) and American bistort (*Polygonum bistortoides*) fill a meadow and mountain ridges reveal a distant view of Mt Olympus.

16 *(left)* The mountain lion or cougar (*Felis concolor*) is North America's largest cat, reaching as much as eight feet in length and 250 lbs in weight. Its nocturnal habits and shy nature, combined with the Peninsula's dense underbrush, ensure that glimpses of this magnificent creature are rare. However it is not uncommon to find cougar tracks on sandbars along any of the major rivers.

17 Olympic chipmunk (*Eutamias amoenus* subsp. *caurinus*), a subspecies of the yellow pine chipmunk, is found only on the Olympic Peninsula in high mountain meadows. Like most chipmunks it hibernates through the winter in small burrows. Seeds and berries form the bulk of its diet, but in many places it is ready and willing to panhandle the hiker.

18 Cascading water rushes down the north fork of the Skokomish River on its journey from the snowfields to the sea.

19 Skunk cabbage (*Lysichitum americanum*) among red alder (*Alnus rubra*). The yellow skunk cabbage is found from Alaska to central California and east to Montana. Both elk and black bear find the skunk cabbage an important spring food source. The plant gets its name from the large, cabbage-like leaves, which give off a pungent smell when bruised or crushed.

20 Olympic marmot (*Marmota olympus*) sunning itself on a rock in an alpine meadow. This relative of the eastern woodchuck is found only in the subalpine and alpine meadows of the Olympics. Though a hibernator, the marmot can often be seen as early as May sitting atop a snowbank through which it has burrowed to rejoin the world. Sunning is a means of gathering vitamin D.

21 *(right)* The great blue heron (*Ardea herodias*) is found across much of North America and is commonly seen in lowland ponds, streams and tidal areas of the Peninsula. Standing over three feet tall, these birds quietly stalk fish, frogs and other aquatic life.

22 A brilliant sunset still lingers in subdued tones as night approaches the
Peninsula's Pacific beaches.

23 Looking west from Grand Peak across mountain ridges that form the
interior of the Olympic mountains.

24 Ski-tracks draw graceful lines down a wintry slope.

25 Morning fog boils out of the valleys near Steeple Rock.

26 *(left)* Two harlequin ducks (*Histrionicus histrionicus*) resting along the Hoh River. These small, rarely seen, sea ducks migrate up freshwater streams in the early spring to court and nest. While they have disappeared from many streams in the Northwest because of pollution and damming, they are still using the pure, fast-flowing rivers of the Peninsula. Both the Hoh and the Elwha rivers afford good occasions to glimpse these strongly marked birds in April and May.

27 Steller's jay (*Cyanocitta stelleri*) is a commonly seen crested bird found west of the Rockies from Alaska to Mexico. Its raucous call is frequently heard in the mountain and lowland forests of the Olympics.

28 Big-leaf maple (*Acer macrophyllum*) draped by moss in the Olympic Rain Forest. Approximately 90 kinds of ferns, mosses and club-mosses grow on trees in these damp forests. Recent studies have concluded that maples send roots into these mats of epiphytes to extract nutrients just as they draw nutrients from the soil of the forest floor. (Epiphytes are plants that live on the surfaces of other plants.)

29 *(right)* Seen in April and May along many of the forest trails among old maple leaves, the evergreen violet (*Viola sempervirens*) is one of several yellow violet species found on the Peninsula.

30 *(left)* Sea-stacks stretch out into the Pacific Ocean at Point of Arches, showing the effects of the relentless struggle between land and sea.

31 Winter fog lying in the Elwha River Valley.

32 The striped skunk (*Mephitis mephitis*) is the most common skunk found across North America. Like most skunk species it is chiefly nocturnal but can sometimes be seen early or late in the day, hunting for mice and insects from farm fields.

33 *(right)* The black bear (*Ursus americanus*) is the only species of bear found on the Peninsula. While in many wild places of North America black bears can be black, brown or cinnamon-colored, in this area only the black color phase is found. Black bears range in all the Olympic habitats from beaches to alpine meadows.

34 *(left)* A subalpine meadow dusted by the first snow of early fall. The red swatches of color are provided by low-growing huckleberry plants.

35 Cattle graze in springtime pastures covered by buttercups near Discovery Bay. Mt Baker of the Cascade Range appears in the distance.

36 *(left)* A Pacific sunset lights cliffs and drift logs near Ruby Beach.

37 An insect's-eye view of bryum moss (*Bryum capillare*) after a spring shower.

38 Big-leaf maple (*Acer macrophyllum*) sporting new spring leaves among sitka spruce (*Picea sitchensis*) along the Quinault River. The Quinault Valley is one of the three major rain-forest river valleys on the west side of the Peninsula. Clouds, heavily laden with moisture, sweep off the Pacific up these valleys and into the Olympics. Rising over the mountains, the clouds shed much of their moisture and the rain-forest valleys average over 140 inches of rain per year.

39 *(right)* Mares with young colts graze in a green spring field near Joyce.

40 Alpenglow bathes the top of Mt Olympus (7,965 feet), the highest point on the Peninsula. The Blue Glacier on the left is one of eight named glaciers on Mt Olympus, the lowest glaciated area in the forty-eight States.

41 Fog settles in the Morse Creek Valley in the Northeast Olympics.

42 Raccoons (*Procyon lotor*) are found across much of the continental US and southern Canada. Mostly nocturnal, they range in brushy or wooded areas near streams, ponds and marshes at low elevations. Likely places for raccoons on the Peninsula are the coastal beaches during low tide, when they feed on mussels and other seafood, and the Heart of the Hills campground, where they make nightly raids on the garbage cans.

43 *(right)* Wood ducks (*Aix sponsa*) are probably the most colorful members of the duck family. They range along the West Coast from southern British Columbia to central California. Although they are not numerous on the Peninsula, their numbers do seem to be growing, helped in some areas by nest boxes provided by local residents.

44 Bracket or shelf fungi (*Polyporus* sp.) are common in the forests of the Peninsula. These relatives of the mushroom grow on tree trunks, exposed roots or fallen logs.

45 *(right)* Avalanche lilies (*Erythronium montanum*) or fawn lilies provide one of the showiest alpine floral displays, forming dense patches of white in both forest and open areas of the Hudsonian Zone, blooming soon after the snow melts. Watch for them in July toward the end of the Obstruction Point road.

46 Evergreen violets (*Viola sempervirens*) in an alder bottom along the upper Soleduck River.

47 A young black-tail fawn on a cold, foggy June morning. Black-tails are
a species of mule deer found on the west side of the Cascade Mountains
from British Columbia to California. During the first few weeks of life
fawns spend much of their time lying motionless on the ground to escape
detection by predators—coyotes, bobcats, cougars and bears.

48 *(left)* Madronas (*Arbutus menziesii*) along the Hood Canal shoreline. These sun-loving relatives of the rhododendron are one of the few broadleaved evergreen trees of the Olympics.

49 Before being extensively trapped for their pelts, river otters (*Lutra canadensis*) were originally found along most water courses in North America. Eating a variety of fish, frogs, crayfish and tidal life, they are commonly observed along the rain-forest rivers and along the coastal shorelines where they are frequently mistaken for their cousins the sea otters.

50 Driftwood marks the tideline along the coast north of Rialto Beach.

51 *(right)* Fisherman repairing his boat in the Port Townsend harbor.

52 A Makah Indian preparing salmon to be baked in a centuries-old tradition during the Makah Days celebration at Neah Bay.

53 City pier, a source of civic pride, in the Port Angeles harbor.

54a A male blue grouse (*Dendragapus obscurus*) performing the mating ritual. Concealed and invisible for most of the year, the yellow air sacs located on both sides of his neck produce a low 'hoooooot' sound during the spring mating season. Hooting blue grouse are frequently sighted along the upper Hurricane Ridge road in May and June.

54b A female blue grouse with young chicks on a cold, foggy morning in an alpine meadow. Blue grouse with young are often seen in late July and August along the trail leading to the top of Hurricane Hill.

54c Douglas squirrel or chickaree (*Tamiasciurus douglasi*) is the only tree squirrel found on the Peninsula. It is a common visitor to many of the forest campgrounds.

54d Black-tail doe washing a young fawn. In the high country, fawns are usually born in June—later in the year than might commonly be expected but suitably so for this harsh environment.

55 *(right)* Mature hemlock forest (*Tsuga heterophylla*) in the upper Soleduck valley.

56 Vine maple (*Acer circinatum*) splashes fall color in the lowland forests of the Peninsula.

57 *(right)* Located in the 'rain shadow' of the Olympics, farms in Dungeness were once world-renowned for butter, hay and seed crops.

58 Female hooded merganser (*Lophodytes cucullatus*) resting in a pond.

59 *(right)* Roosevelt elk (*Cervis elaphus*) on a misty morning along the Hoh River. Much of what is now Olympic National Park was first set aside as a National Monument in 1909 by Theodore Roosevelt (for whom this sub-species of elk is named) to help preserve a dwindling elk population. Elk are now frequently seen along the Elwha, Hoh, Queets and Quinault river roads and by hikers in the Olympic backcountry.

60 Bald eagle (*Haliaeetus levcocephalus*) feeding on a steelhead. Bald eagles are year-round inhabitants of the Peninsula, with a number of protected nesting sites. Winter is the best time to observe eagles, as many migrants come south from Alaska and Canada to winter along the coast and feed on spawned-out salmon along the rivers. One place to view these wintering eagles is at the junction of Highway 101 and the Hamma Hamma River.

61 *(right)* Long-billed dowitchers (*Limnodromus scolopaceus*) pause in Grays Harbor during the northernly spring migration. A wide variety of shore birds use the Grays Harbor area in the spring as a staging area to gorge on the rich supply of saltwater organisms, fattening for the long flight to nesting grounds in the Arctic.

62 Steep, forested slopes frame the Dosewallips River in May.

63 *(right)* A derelict apple orchard blooming along the Dosewallips road. Forgotten orchards bear silent testimony to the optimism of early settlers.

64 Log ship in Port Angeles harbor. Exporting logs to Asian markets is an important part of the Peninsula's economy.

65 Abandoned sawmill at Maynard on Discovery Bay.

66 A view of Port Angeles tucked into the foothills of the Olympics. Log ships lie at anchor in the harbor.

67 *(right)* Coastline of the Strait of Juan de Fuca seen from the Salt Creek recreation area.

68 Shucking oysters at low tide along Hood Canal.

69 *(right)* Surf-fishing near Kalaloch.

70 Coastline north of Kalaloch. The Olympic Peninsula coast is the only wilderness shoreline left in the continental US outside Alaska.

71 *(right)* Fishing boats moored in the Hoquiam River. Salmon fishing has long been vital to the area's economy.

72–73 *(overleaf)* Sunrise from the Morse Creek observation point with Puget Sound, Fidalgo Island and Mt Baker in the distance. Dungeness Spit in the lower right foreground is one of the longest natural spits in the world.

74 Fishermen dipping surf smelt at Beach #4 north of Kalaloch.

75 Found along the coast from Alaska to Baja California, black oyster-catchers (*Haematopus bachmani*) use their bills to open mussels and to pry limpets from surf-pounded rocks. The presence of these shy birds is a sign that the ecosystem of a shoreline remains intact and undisturbed.

76 *(left)* Sports fishermen mooching for salmon in the Strait of Juan de Fuca against the backdrop of Vancouver Island.

77 The Olympic mountains seen on a winter morning from south Seattle.

78 Wild strawberries (*Fragaria* sp.) are found on old river bars, along roadsides in the lower elevation forests and on bluffs overlooking the ocean.

79 *(right)* Nurse log in the Olympic rain-forest. A foothold of nutrients and moisture, an anchorage for growing seedlings, this nurse log will eventually decompose, leaving a proud colonnade of rain forest trees.

80 Calypso orchids (*Calypso bulbosa*), named for the goddess in Homer's *Odyssey,* thrive in the darkness of moist, coniferous forests in late spring.

81 *(right)* Spreading phlox (*Phlox diffusa*) rimed with hoar-frost, a delightful alpine flower of the Olympics.

82 *(left)* Snowfields linger into summer on these high ridges southwest of Hayden Pass.

83 Black-tail buck chews American bistort (*Polygonum bistortoides*) on a meadowed slope of Hurricane Hill.

84 *(left)* Wet sand reflects sunset and sea-stacks at Second Beach near LaPush.

85 Wind-scoured fir trees frame a Pacific sunset.

86 Completed in 1890 in the Romanesque style, the Port Townsend courthouse is one of the earliest brick structures on the Peninsula. The bricks were baked in St Louis, the sandstone was quarried in Alaska, the bells for the tower's clocks were forged in Boston and sent overland by ox-cart. A similar story attaches to each of the numerous historic buildings that grace the area.

87 *(right)* An unnamed alpine tarn reflects the sunset over Mt Olympus.

88 Early morning in April on Lake Crescent, Olympic National Park.